A Picn in the Rain

by Sharon Fear
illustrated by John Bendall-Brunello

Moosling

Rabbit wanted
to have a picnic.
But it was raining.

Rabbit saw Mouse.
"I don't like the rain,"
he said.

"Come and sit under my umbrella," said Mouse.

But the umbrella was too small.

Mouse wanted to have
a picnic with Rabbit.
But it was raining.

They saw Skunk.
"We don't like the rain,"
said Rabbit.

"Come sit in my tent," said Skunk.

But the tent was much too small.

Skunk wanted
to have a picnic
with Mouse and Rabbit.
But it was raining **hard**.

They saw Moosling.
"We want
to have a picnic,
but we don't like
the rain," Rabbit said.

"Do you have
a big tent, Moosling?"
said Skunk.

"No, I don't have
a tent," Moosling said.

"Do you have
a big umbrella?"
said Mouse.

"No, I don't have
a big umbrella,"
said Moosling.

"But **I** am big," he said.
"I like the rain.
And I **love** picnics!
Come and sit under me!"

And they did.